Summertime Math

by Amy Ayers
Illustrations by Lorin Walter

Developed for Harcourt, Inc., by Gareth Stevens, Inc. This edition published by Harcourt, Inc., by agreement with Gareth Stevens, Inc. No part of this publication may be reproduced or transmitted in any form or by any means, electronic or mechanical, including photocopy, recording, or any information storage and retrieval system, without permission in writing from the copyright holder.

Requests for permission to make copies of any part of the work should be addressed to Permissions Department, Gareth Stevens, Inc., 330 West Olive Street, Suite 100, Milwaukee, Wisconsin 53212. Fax: 414-332-3567.

HARCOURT and the Harcourt Logo are trademarks of Harcourt, Inc., registered in the United States of America and/or other jurisdictions.

Printed in China

ISBN 13: 978-0-15-360218-4
ISBN 10: 0-15-360218-X

11 12 0940 16 15 14
4500514402

Harcourt
SCHOOL PUBLISHERS

It is summer!
I visit the beach.

I can do math at the beach.

I count many things.

I count 8 big umbrellas.

I count 15 birds.

They fly in the sky over the sea.

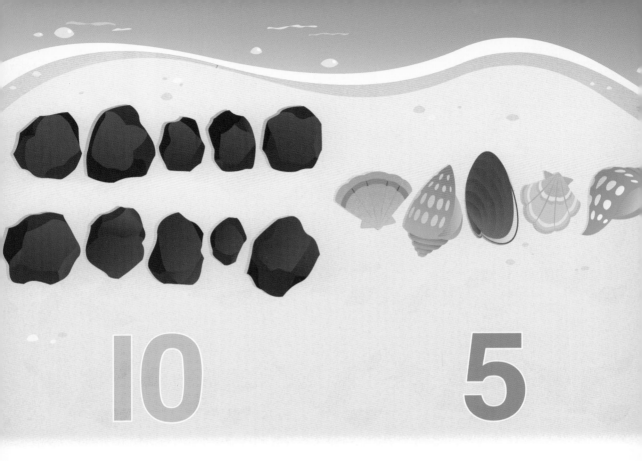

I see rocks and shells.
There are more rocks than shells.

6

3

7

I see shovels and pails.

There are fewer shovels than pails.

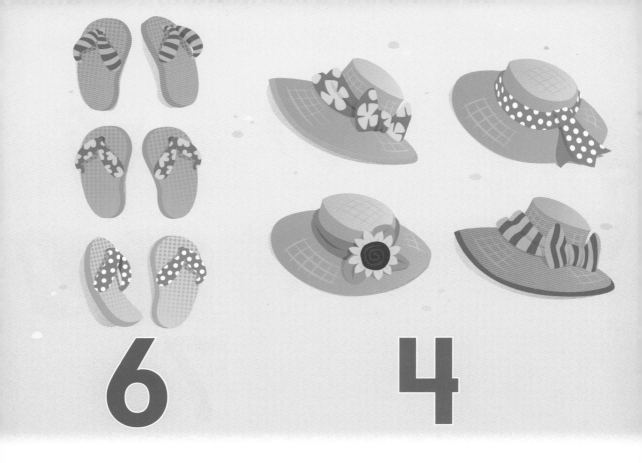

I see sandals and hats.

There are more sandals than hats.

8

I see 2 big birds. I see 2 small birds.
I see 4 birds in all.

1

4

I see 1 green pail. I see 4 blue pails.
I see 5 pails in all.

Math at the beach is fun!

Glossary

fewer

more

sandal

shovel

umbrella